The magic of
the Highlands

Books by W. A. Poucher
available from Constable

Scotland
Wales
The Lake District
The Highlands of Scotland
The Alps
The Yorkshire Dales
* and the Peak District*
Lakeland fells
The West Country
Skye
Ireland
The magic of Skye
The Scottish Peaks
The Peak and Pennines
The Lakeland Peaks
The Welsh Peaks

Other books now out of print

The backbone of England
Climbing with a camera
Escape to the hills
A camera in the Cairngorms
Scotland through the lens
Highland holiday
The North Western Highlands
Lakeland scrapbook
Lakeland through the lens
Lakeland holiday
Lakeland journey
Over lakeland fells
Wanderings in Wales
Snowdonia through the lens
Snowdon holiday
Peak panorama
The Surrey hills
The magic of the Dolomites
West country journey
Journey into Ireland

THE MAGIC OF THE HIGHLANDS

W. A. Poucher

Constable London

First published in Great Britain 1987
by Constable and Company Limited
10 Orange Street London WC2H 7EG
Copyright © 1987 by W.A. Poucher
ISBN 0 09 467810 3
Text filmset by Servis Filmsetting Ltd, Manchester
Printed and bound in Japan by
Dai Nippon Company, Tokyo

The Photographs

Preface

In the many years that I spent when I was younger climbing and photographing peaks all over the British Isles and in several other mountainous areas of the world, I fell in love with countless wild areas of scenic beauty. But my favourite landscape remains the Scottish Highlands and the misty Isle of Skye, and I returned to these again and again, to climb the hills I loved best and capture on film the breathtaking panoramas from their summits. This is my fourth book of colour pictures of that glorious country.

I am often asked, 'What is the best time to visit and photograph the Scottish hills?' The answer is twofold: spring in general is my preferred season, for during the months of April and May a limpid atmosphere and fine cumulus are frequent occurrences, and so less time is wasted in waiting for favourable lighting. Moreover, during April many of the higher mountains are dressed in snowy raiment which adds sparkle and Alpine glamour to the pictures. But the end of October is also an excellent time for photography, for then the dying bracken turns a fiery red, the grass is golden yellow, and longer shadows increase the contrast between ben and glen. Lighting is the key to successful mountain photography: if possible avoid exposures at midday when the overhead light is flat and uninteresting; choose instead early morning or evening, when the sunlight, slanting at an angle of 45 degrees over your shoulder, will yield the most interesting contrasts.

There is no greater satisfaction than attaining the summit cairn on one of Scotland's great peaks, inhaling the invigorating mountain air and scanning the glens far below, captivated by the spirit and mystery of the hills. But in many parts of Scotland, particularly in the Cairngorms, the peaks are often a very great distance from the nearest road or starting point, and you may first have to walk over vast stretches of rough moorland, often dappled with bog. The climbs themselves are often long and arduous, so good planning, an early start, and the company of at least two others are essential for safety. Anyone who ventures out on the hills without proper equipment and sufficient forethought is asking for trouble. I have generally indicated in this book those peaks which may be attempted by walkers, and those which are the preserve of the experienced climber: for full details of the safe ascent of all the mountains pictured herein, I refer readers to my *Scottish peaks*.

The photographs are arranged in sequence, starting with the Firth of Clyde in the West and proceeding northwards (with a diversion to the beautiful island of Skye) through the North-western Highlands and Sutherland, before circling south again to the Cairngorms and the Grampians. Visitors to Scotland can thus follow my route, either by car or on foot, and marvel at these unforgettable vistas for themselves.

W.A. Poucher
1987

Ailsa Craig and the Firth of Clyde

Jutting sharply up from the sea, Ailsa Craig is
an unmistakable landmark for sailors. The rock
from Ailsa Craig has been used for many years
to make curling stones.

On Goat Fell

The Arran hills give splendid days out for the hill-walker. Goat Fell, the highest point on the island, is easily reached from Brodick, the landing-place for most visitors from the mainland. The hill and surrounding area, together with Brodick Castle (now a Country Park) are owned by the National Trust for Scotland.

Brodick Bay from Goat Fell

(overleaf)

The climb on to the southern ridge of Goat Fell, Arran's highest peak at 2,870 feet, reveals this extensive panorama of Brodick Bay, with the conical hill of Mullach Mor on Holy Island beyond.

Glen Sannox from North Goat Fell

The view north-east down Glen Sannox, with
Mullach Buidhe on the right, shows the wild
nature of the landscape in the heart of the Arran
hills.

Looking up Glen Sannox

(overleaf)

Glen Sannox, a few miles north of Brodick, is enclosed by high, steep hills. The north ridge, prominent in this photograph, includes the famous Leum Caillich (the Witch's Step) and terminates in the fine peak of Cir Mhor.

Cioch na h-Oige from Sannox

(overleaf pp 22/23)

The steep ridge of Cioch na h-Oige soars from the farmland and moor on the south side of Glen Sannox. It provides an interesting alternative route to the summit of Goat Fell, of which it is an outlier.

Lochranza Castle

The coast road round the north of Arran leads
to Lochranza, with its small bay and castle. The
peninsula of Kintyre can be seen in the distance.

Ben Lomond from Loch Lomond

Less than an hour's drive from Glasgow, Ben
Lomond broods peacefully over its shining loch,
the most famous in Scotland. A well-trodden
track provides easy ascent of this southernmost
'Munro' (or 3,000-ft peak), from Rowardennan
on Loch Lomond's eastern shore.

The Cobbler — North Peak

(overleaf)

Two views of the serrated profile of The Cobbler (or Ben Arthur, to give it its proper name): the North Peak, which resembles a cobbler's last, is the most easily attainable by walkers, but the whole mountain, rising above the village of Arrochar, is a popular haunt of rock-climbers.

Overhang of the North Peak

Jutting out like the prow of a great ship, this spectacular overhang displays the characteristic ripples of volcanic rock from which The Cobbler is sculpted.

Loch Fyne and Inveraray

(overleaf)

Inveraray is the ancient home of the Clan Campbell. The present village dates from 1746 and is a fine example of eighteenth-century town planning. The unusual large white gateways add to the tidy and attractive appearance of the village.

Main street, Inveraray

In summer this pretty village becomes very busy
indeed, with a festive atmosphere about it.
Inveraray is world-famous for Loch Fyne
kippers.

Inveraray Castle

(overleaf)

The castle is a striking square edifice with round towers at each corner and an extra tower in the middle. Home of the present Duke of Argyll, the building replaces an earlier castle of the fifteenth century, whose ruins can still be seen.

Gateway to the Isles

Oban is both a holiday centre and an important
ferry-terminal for those travelling to the Isle of
Mull. In summertime its streets are busy with
holidaymakers.

Cruachan from across Loch Awe

(overleaf)

The blue waters of Loch Awe make a fine foreground to the majesty of Ben Cruachan, rearing 3,689 feet into the sky. The loch, almost twenty-five miles in length, is the longest in Scotland.

Cruachan and the Dalmally Horseshoe

(overleaf pp 42/43)

Stob Daimh, one of Cruachan's many peaks, lies close to the eastern end of the main massif, at the apex of an east-facing curve of peaks and ridges: the Dalmally Horseshoe. The circuit of these peaks makes a good day out, over comparatively easy terrain.

Cruachan from near the village of Taynuilt

(overleaf pp 44/45)

Ben Cruachan dominates the rich farmlands of Lorn in mid-Argyll. In this picture Stob Dearg (3,611 feet) raises its lofty head above the village which gives it its nickname – the Taynuilt Peak.

The Taynuilt Peak

This view looks west towards Stob Dearg, or the Taynuilt Peak of Cruachan, beyond which gleam the blue waters of the Firth of Lorn and the distant hills of Morvern.

The view from the summit

(overleaf)

A magnificent prospect greets the climber who has reached the top of Cruachan. The view north sweeps up the length of Loch Etive, past Ben Starav, to the Glencoe hills and Ben Nevis on the horizon.

Cruachan

As is seen here, this mountain, one of the finest and best-known in Scotland, is a complex massif. Leaving the main peak and descending towards Drochaid Glas, the ridge running in from the right is the Stob Garbh-Stob Daimh ridge.

Cruachan
from Blackmount

(overleaf)

North of Cruachan, the country is dominated by the marvellous hills of the Blackmount deer forest. A magnificent, long, low-level walk can be taken through delectable mountain scenery from Inveroran to Loch Etive by Glen Kinglass.

The Pass of Brander from Cruachan

This picture was taken on the slopes of Meall
Cuanail of Cruachan, looking down on the
precipitous Pass of Brander. The waters of Loch
Awe are harnessed in this narrow gorge and
used for hydro-electric power.

The Pass of Brander

(overleaf)

Where the River Awe flows from Loch Awe through the gorge, the steep rocky walls of the Pass force river, road and railway to run side by side.

Kilchurn Castle and Ben Lui from across Loch Awe

Sitting on its marshy headland, Kilchurn Castle
has an atmosphere of gauntness and aloofness. It
is the ancient home of the Campbells of
Breadalbane, and is open to visitors in the
summer season.

Ben Lui

(overleaf)

There is no finer sight in the Central Highlands than the twin tops of Ben Lui, garbed in winter white. The key for climbers approaching from Tyndrum is Cononish Farm, just visible here towards the lower right of the picture. A sporting route goes up the left ridge of the huge corrie.

The north ridge of Ben Lui

An unusual view of this fine peak, normally photographed from its eastern side when the twin peaks of its summit and the great corrie beneath them are visible. Mature forestry, seen here in its infancy, now mars the ascent of the north ridge.

Beinn Dorain

Climbing out of Tyndrum to the great Moor of
Rannoch along the A82, the motorist is struck
by this view of the shapely cone of Beinn
Dorain, whose steep slopes rear sheer to the sky
from Auch Glen. A rewarding ascent begins at
Bridge of Orchy via Coire an Dothaidh.

The Inveroran Inn

(overleaf)

Renowned as a place where William and
Dorothy Wordsworth once stayed, this isolated
hostelry is a favourite with climbers seeking
access to the Blackmount peaks which border
the road across Rannoch Moor to Glencoe.

Sron na Creise from Rannoch Moor

Usually climbed in conjunction with its neighbour, Meall a' Bhuiridh, to give an entertaining day, this peak lies to the south of Glen Etive which divides it from the sheer ramparts of the Buachaille Etive Mor to the north of the glen. The adventurous can scramble up its northern side to gain the top – more forgiving than it appears here, frowning across the autumn glory of Rannoch Moor.

Blackmount
from Rannoch Moor
(overleaf)

As the A82 climbs over the wild expanse of
Rannoch Moor it gives fine views westwards to
the Blackmount hills. The major peak to the left
of this view is Stob Ghabhar (peak of the goats)
and in the centre of the picture is Coire Ba, one
of the largest and grandest in the Highlands.

Buachaille Etive Mor

A bend in the road running north to Fort
William reveals this breathtaking view of the
Buachaille Etive Mor. The main peak, Stob
Dearg, is in fact the culmination of a long ridge
containing three other peaks: Stob na Doire,
Stob Coire Altruim and Stob na Broige.

Buachaille Etive Mor from Kingshouse

(overleaf)

A superb view of the 'Great Herdsman of Etive', from the old hostelry of Kingshouse, which lies on the old Glencoe road and which is an excellent centre from which climbers and walkers can pit their strength against the Buachaille and its neighbours.

The Three Sisters of Glencoe

(overleaf pp 76/77)

At the top of the descent into the Pass of Glencoe this grand view greets the traveller. The peaks of Glencoe contain the highest mountains in Argyll and are not for the average walker.

The gorge in Glencoe

The new road through Glencoe, built in the
1930s, was a great feat of engineering that
blasted its way through sheer walls of rock.
Today's visitors enjoy the benefits of this road,
as they drive through the pass with prospects of
superb grandeur on either side.

Aonach Eagach
and Ben Nevis

(overleaf)

The spectacular ridge of Aonach Eagach is one of the narrowest and most exciting on the mainland of Scotland, and is the domain of the experienced mountain scrambler. All exertion is amply rewarded with the first distant views of the Mamores and Ben Nevis.

The Aonach Eagach from Am Bodach

This is the starting point of the traverse of the
sensational Aonach Eagach ridge. Once on it,
there is no escape from it until you have reached
the last peak, Sgorr nam Fiannaidh.

Approaching the most difficult section of the ridge

The narrowest and most precipitous section of the Aonach Eagach ridge lies between Meall Dearg and Stob Leith, where it becomes a series of pinnacles and arêtes.

Pinnacles on the ridge

This picture shows one of the tricky sections on the ridge where the walker has to use hands as well as feet. This pinnacle is negotiated by way of a narrow chimney which takes the walker on to an airy crest.

Loch Achtriochtan from the Aonach Eagach

(overleaf)

Looking down into the depths of Glencoe from high on Am Bodach, the climber can make out the Fort William road passing the shores of Loch Achtriochtan, said to be the lair of a kelpie, or water-horse!

Stob Coire nan Lochan

(overleaf pp 90/91)

Looking towards the south side of Glencoe from the Aonach Eagach ridge, you see this superb view of Stob Coire nan Lochan whose summit is lifted high by its two outliers, Gearr Aonach and Aonach Dubh.

Looking back towards Am Bodach

(overleaf pp 92/93)

Behind Am Bodach, as the climber pauses on the Aonach Eagach ridge, he can see the distinctive shape of the Buachaille Etive Mor in the blue distance: a truly breath-taking vista.

A rugged prospect

The hills of the Bidean nam Bian massif are characterised by bleak and rocky flanks, which make it a serious challenge to hill-walkers and climbers. This is Stob Coire nam Beith, seen from its outlier, An t-Sron.

Glencoe and Loch Leven

(overleaf)

This picture is taken looking down towards Glencoe village from An t-Sron. The narrow Pass of Glencoe has widened out into a broad strath and from the sea Loch Leven bites deeply inland. Beyond the loch lie the rugged hills of Ardgour, Garbh Bheinn being the highest. This picture was taken before the Ballachulish bridge was built.

The Lochaber hills

(overleaf pp 98/99)

From the summit of An t-Sron on the south side of Glencoe, the view north takes in the 'notched ridge' of the Aonach Eagach, the Mamores and the snow-flecked summit of Ben Nevis: a stupendous panorama that is irresistible to any mountain photographer.

Loch Leven and the Pap of Glencoe

(overleaf pp 100/101)

Instead of using the new road bridge at Ballachulish, it is well worth driving round this glorious sea loch, through the village of Kinlochleven. The older road offers a succession of lovely views of the surrounding hills, including the Pap of Glencoe, western outlier of the Aonach Eagach ridge.

Loch Leven and the hills of Ardgour

The still waters of Loch Leven perfectly mirror
the faraway hills of Ardgour. It is not often that
the Highland scene is as sweetly sunlit as this –
the area has one of the highest rainfall figures
for the whole of Britain!

Ben Nevis and the Mamores

(overleaf)

Viewed from above Glen Etive, the familiar shape of Britain's highest mountain, Ben Nevis, appears at the far left of the photograph. In the middle distance is the magnificent Mamores range, a full traverse of which is one of the great hill days of Scotland.

Ben Nevis from Banavie

Sunshine highlights the rugged profile of the monarch of Britain's peaks, which is estimated to have only about twenty clear days a year! If you are lucky enough to reach the summit on one of those days, your view across the encircling hills will be unsurpassed, for you will be standing more than 4,400 feet above sea level.

Loch Laggan and Binnein Shuas

(overleaf)

The dark mass of Binnein Shuas broods behind the still waters of Loch Laggan against a thundery sky, the sombreness of the scene being relieved by the brilliant autumn colours in the foreground. Though large parts of the Highlands nowadays are covered with commercial pine forests, broad-leaved gems like the trees in the picture still add glorious hues to the landscape, and delight the photographer.

Creag Meagaidh

(overleaf pp 110/111)

The large mass of this mountain to the west of Loch Laggan looks rather unexceptional from the lochside road. But the motorist prepared to leave the car and don a pair of walking boots can see its hidden gem – the spectacular Coire Ardair, attained after a fair walk along an often boggy track.

Coire Ardair

The precipices of this rocky corrie on Creag Meagaidh offer particularly fine winter climbing routes of all grades. This picture shows the three 'Posts' or gullies, and their attendant buttresses, across the lochan that nestles at the foot of the towering crags.

The Glencoe hills from Ardgour

(overleaf)

Crossing Loch Linnhe by the Corran ferry and driving south for a few miles revealed this perfect view back, across the rippling water, towards Glencoe. The Pap of Glencoe is clearly visible, with the Aonach Eagach ridge leading away from it.

Garbh Bheinn

(overleaf pp 116/117)

'The rough hill' (Garbh Bheinn) is well named, as this picture reveals. The full traverse of the mountain gives an exhilarating day, and the view from its summit is outstanding. The little lochan, reflecting the sky, makes a perfect foreground for this study.

Garbh Bheinn across Coire an Iubhair

The fine ridge running north-west to the
summit of Garbh Bheinn is seen to advantage
here, as are the mountain's slabby eastern slopes.

The view up
Loch Sunart

(overleaf)

This is one of the longest, finest, and wildest sea lochs on Scotland's western seaboard, and yields many very fine views. Looking eastwards up the loch, the grey bulk of Garbh Bheinn dominates the scene and acts as a natural focus for the photographer.

Loch Shiel

(overleaf pp 122|123)

Loch Shiel cuts through the hills for nearly twenty miles, from its head at Glenfinnan to its foot near the village of Acharacle, where this photograph was taken. The prominent peak in the centre right distance is Sgurr Dhomhnuill (Donald's Peak), which rises to nearly 3,000 feet.

The Glenfinnan
Monument

(overleaf pp 124|125)

There can be few more familiar scenes in the Highlands of Scotland than this one – the monument to Prince Charles Edward Stuart at the head of Loch Shiel. The monument is owned by the National Trust for Scotland, and their Visitors Centre nearby tells the story of the Prince and the 1745 Rising which he led.

The birch-clad shores of Loch Benevian

Close to Glen Affric lie the tranquil waters of
Loch Benevian. The Forestry Commission has
managed successfully to protect and integrate
the native birches and ancient Caledonian pines.
A public right-of-way starts west of here and
leads the walker through magnificent Glen
Affric to Kintail.

Eilean Donan Castle

(overleaf)

One of Scotland's most easily recognisable fortresses, Eilean Donan is sited alongside the road to the Kyle of Lochalsh, gateway to Skye. It was blown up in 1719 by an English warship after the battle of Glen Shiel, but subsequently restored. The castle's situation on Loch Shiel, as seen here, is truly majestic, and a fitting memorial to Clan MacRae.

Skye from Applecross

Looking west from the Applecross peninsula there is an uninterrupted view of the magical 'Misty Isle'. In this picture, Skye's spectacular Black Cuillin ridge is seen in the background, lightly dusted with snow.

Basalt sea cliffs

(overleaf)

Skye consists partly of the roughest rock in Britain, gabbro – loved by climbers for its superb friction – and partly of basalt which is treacherous when wet. These vertical cliffs, looking for all the world like organ pipes, are a feature of the Skye coastline.

The Storr rocks

The north-eastern corner of the island, in the Trotternish district, harbours some weird and wonderful rock formations set amongst wild and untamed moorland. The Old Man of Storr, one of the best known, is among the pinnacles viewed here from a distance. A circular tour of The Storr ridge brings the walker into close proximity with them and offers fine prospects across the Sound of Raasay to the mainland peaks.

Further north still from The Storr lies another
fantastic group of towers and buttresses. Most
climbers visiting Skye tend to concentrate on
the Cuillin ridge, but the journey north through
Portree to Quiraing can be equally rewarding,
especially for devotees of the unusual.

View from the Table

Hidden away in the uppermost recesses of Quiraing is an oval platform known as the Table. If you are fortunate enough to climb to it on a fine day, such as the one on which this photograph was taken, you will revel in vistas of distant seas and close-ups of the strange rock formations at hand.

Dunvegan Castle

(overleaf)

Seat of the Macleod chiefs for more than seven centuries, this uncompromising building with a few exterior embellishments is set imposingly on a rock with the sea on three sides. Once it was reached only by boat or a subterranean passage: today access is by bridge.

Duntulm Castle, Trotternish

(overleaf pp 144/145)

Perched high on a cliff overlooking the sea, the reputedly haunted ruins echo the bizarre rock formations of The Storr and Quiraing. Of old it was a seat of the Macdonald Lords of the Isles.

Liathach

This is the classic view from Loch Clair of the truly magnificent sandstone giant, Liathach. The climber does well to treat with respect its airy ridge under snow – the main problem is the serrated pinnacles of Am Fasarinen which must be negotiated with extreme care if the climber wishes to avoid hurtling hundreds of feet into the wild corries below.

Mullach an Rathain across Loch Torridon

(overleaf)

The peak, one of Liathach's two 'Munros', towers above the new youth hostel at Torridon. This picture clearly shows the great gash which splits the front of the peak, and also reveals effectively the distinctive sandstone terraces on the right that make up this mighty mountain.

Coire Mhic Nobuil and Beinn Alligin

(overleaf pp 150/151)

The wild reaches of this glen, with its babbling burn tumbling down to meet Loch Torridon, are a perfect vantage-point for the great northern corries of Liathach and the delightful profile of Beinn Alligin, 'jewel of Torridon'. The 'Horns' of Alligin are visible on the skyline directly behind the bridge.

Beinn Eighe from Liathach

Largest of the three Torridonian giants in terms of sheer mass, Beinn Eighe is a complete range in itself. Its vast quartzite screes, seen here, guard one of the finest sights in all Scotland for the mountaineer – Coire Mhic Fhearchair, reached after a lengthy trek from Glen Torridon, which contains the breathtaking spectacle of the huge Triple Buttress of A'Choinneach Mhor.

Beinn Eighe from Glen Torridon

(overleaf)

The start of the walk into Coire Mhic Fhearchair is a car-park at the foot of Coire Dubh, the corrie dividing the eastern ramparts of Liathach from Beinn Eighe. Not far from the car-park, this ruin makes a popular camp-site.

Bealach na Ba and Loch Kishorn

The road from Tornapress climbs over 2,000
feet in a distance of only six miles, to reach this
lofty bealach; a twisting drive ending in a series
of zigzags at a gradient of 1:4. From the car-
park at the summit the view is superb, with a
splendid distant prospect of the peaks of Rum
and Skye.

The Applecross hills from Kishorn Lodge

(overleaf)

The snowy ramparts of these hills rear up against the sky on the road to Shieldaig, two miles north of Tornapress. Facing north-east, the four great corries of Beinn Bhan, each separated by a castellated spur, have sheer walls plunging vertically for some 1,500 feet. A stalkers' track leaves the river bridge at Tornapress, crossing rough heath and boulders to reach the corries.

Highland bridge

(overleaf pp 160/161)

Stone bridges dot the Scottish Highlands and are an indispensable aid to walkers when the rivers become roaring torrents after heavy rain. Many of the bridges were built by General Wade, whose roads also figure prominently on the maps.

Looking down on Coire na Poite

A three-mile tramp over springy moorland from
Bealach na Ba brings one to the summit of
Beinn Bhan, and the dizzying bird's-eye view of
the gleaming green lochans cradled in the depths
of the great corrie, far below.

A distant view of Stac Polly

(overleaf)

A few miles north of Ullapool, on the road to Elphin, lies this exquisite lochan, which perfectly sets off the blue outlines of Stac Polly, Cul Mor, and Cul Beag.

Sgurr an Fhidhlair from Lochan Tuath

The great prow of Sgurr an Fhidhlair, on the north side of Ben More Coigach, rises for over 1,000 feet from the side of Lochan Tuath, a rough three-mile walk from the nearest road.

Cul Mor from Stac Polly

(overleaf)

The extraordinary mountains of western Sutherland, rising as they do from a vast watery plain, form a landscape of quite distinctive and intriguing appearance.

Suilven from Cul Mor

Suilven presents two very different aspects, for
the famous prow which is disclosed from the
Elphin road hides a long serrated ridge behind it
– revealed (as seen in this picture) from the
vantage-point of Cul Mor.

Sandwood Bay

(overleaf)

The great sweep of Sandwood Bay, two miles
long, lies some twelve miles south of Cape
Wrath, which is the north-westernmost tip of
Scotland. The bay, which can only be reached
on foot, has a wonderful atmosphere of
remoteness and peace.

A sparkling sea

(overleaf pp 174/175)

With something over 3,000 miles of coastline,
Scotland offers many variations on the theme of
water, sun, cliff and sand. The northern and
eastern coasts are particularly blessed with
enchanting coastal scenery featuring all these.

Limestone caves

The sea's endless interaction with the land
creates shapes and forms of extraordinary
variety. Driven by the prevailing westerly wind,
the pounding waves scour cliff and rock, and
since limestone is particularly vulnerable to
erosion, caves and arches can be found all along
this seaboard.

The Lairig Ghru from Rothiemurchus

(overleaf)

The Lairig Ghru, the great trench that splits the Cairngorms in two, is one of the most famous passes in Scotland. Here it is revealed from the Rothiemurchus Forest, on the Aviemore side.

The northern corries from Loch Morlich

(overleaf pp 180/181)

The shores of Loch Morlich, on the road between Aviemore and the Cairngorm ski-slopes, command an unsurpassed view of the northern corries of Cairngorm. From left to right they are Coire Cas, Coire an t'Sneachda and Coire an Lochain. The area has been the centre of a storm of controversy in recent years over the extent of development for ski-ing.

The cliffs of Coire an t' Sneachda

At the head of this fine corrie, its cliffs are
topped by a broad plateau that links Cairngorm
and Ben Macdui – the largest expanse of land at
more than 4,000 feet in Britain. In the centre of
the picture is Aladdin's Couloir, a famous snow
and ice climb.

Cairn Lochan

(overleaf)

The Cairngorms provide vistas of rugged mountain grandeur, as here at the summit of Coire an Lochain, which is just a few feet short of the 4,000-ft mark. The Cairn can be attained easily by walking from the summit of Cairngorm, which itself is only 500 feet above the top station on the chairlift. The upper slopes of Coire an Lochain are prone to avalanches, and many accidents have occurred here.

Loch Avon from Ben Macdui

(overleaf pp 186/187)

In the heart of the Cairngorms, and at a height of more than 2,000 feet, Loch Avon is frozen for several months of each year. In this photograph, however, it glimmers under cloudy summer skies, with Beinn Mheadhoin and its strange summit tors rising beyond the loch's southern (right) shore.

Lochnagar from the Spittal of Glenmuick

The cliffs above the waters of Lochnagar offer rock climbing of all grades, but walkers can make for the summit of Lochnagar mountain. The most popular routes start from a car-park and small visitors' centre at the end of a road running up Glen Muick from Ballater. The whole area is a nature reserve, and is part of the Balmoral estate owned by the royal family.

A hill burn

(overleaf)

The tumbling waters of the hill burn provide the mountain wanderer with refreshment at the beginning and end of the day. Many is the time I have sat by such a burn to reflect on the day's adventures and to plan for the morrow.

The Queen's View, Loch Tummel

The magnificent peak of Schiehallion (3,547
feet) dominates the scenery of central Perthshire,
the ancient lands of Breadalbane. A parking
place on the B8019 road a few miles out of
Pitlochry commands the 'Queen's View' seen
here, which is named after a visit made by
Queen Victoria in 1866. The eye is drawn down
the lovely length of Loch Tummel to the peak
rearing up against the distant skyline.

Schiehallion

(overleaf)

Loch Rannoch is ten miles long and the centre
of an outstandingly beautiful area. Looking
eastwards, Schiehallion appears as a perfect
cone, framed by the trees. Its shape led to the
mountain's being used by Maskelyne, an
eighteenth-century Astronomer Royal, in
experiments to determine the mass of the earth.

Ben Lawers from Loch Tay

(overleaf pp 196/197)

A sweeping ridge of hills, which are mostly
grassy and a wonderful place to wander, guards
Loch Tay's north-western shore. In the centre of
this is Ben Lawers, highest mountain in the
Southern Highlands, and renowned for its
beautiful alpine flora.

A Highland sunset

(overleaf pp 198/199)

The Highlands' combination of mountains,
water, and seemingly endless skies, is magical as
the sun sinks to rest after a long summer
evening. I always make every effort to capture
such moments of glory: they remain in the
memory – and on film – as a treasure for ever.